If the days of creation are really geologic ages of millions of years, then the gospel message is undermined at its foundation because it puts death, disease, thorns, and suffering *before* the Fall. This idea also shows an erroneous approach to Scripture—that the Word of God can be interpreted on the basis of the fallible theories of sinful people.

It is a good exercise to read Genesis chapter 1 and try to put aside outside influences that may cause you to have a predetermined idea of what the word "day" may mean. Just let the words of the passage speak to you.

Taking Genesis 1 in this way, at face value, without doubt says that God created the universe, the earth, the sun, moon and stars, plants and animals, and the first two people within six ordinary (approximately 24-hour) days. Being really honest, you would have to admit that you could never get the idea of millions of years from reading this passage.

The majority of Christians (including many Christian leaders) in the Western world, however, either do not insist that these days of creation were ordinary-length days or they accept and teach that they must have been long periods of time—even millions or billions of years.

How does God communicate to us?

God communicates through language. When He made the first man, Adam, He had already "programmed" him with a language, so there could be communication. Human language consists of words used in a specific context that relates to the entire reality around us.

Thus, God can reveal things to man, and man can communicate with God, as these words have meaning and convey an understandable message. If this were not so, how could any of us communicate with each other, or with God, or God with us?

Why "long days"?

Romans 3:4 declares: "Let God be true, and every man a liar."

In *every* instance where someone has not accepted the "days" of creation to be ordinary days, it is because they have *not* allowed the words of Scripture to speak to them in context, as the language requires for communication. They have been influenced by ideas from *outside* of Scripture. Thus, they have set a precedent that could allow any word to be reinterpreted by the preconceived ideas of the person reading the words. Ultimately, this will lead to a communication breakdown, as the same words in the same context could mean different things to different people.

The church fathers. Most "church fathers" accepted the days as ordinary days.[1] It is true that some of the early church fathers did not teach the "days" of creation as ordinary days—but many of them had been influenced by Greek philosophy, which caused them to interpret the days as allegorical. They reasoned that the creation "days" were related to God's activities, and God being timeless meant that the "days" could not be related to human time.[2] In contrast to today's allegorizers, they could not accept that God took *as long as* six days.

Thus, the non-literal "days" resulted from extra-biblical influences (i.e., influences *outside* the Bible), not from the words of the Bible!

This approach has affected the way people interpret Scripture to this day. As the man who started the Reformation said:

> The days of creation were ordinary days in length. We must understand that these days were actual days *(veros dies),* contrary to the opinion of the Holy Fathers. Whenever we observe that the opinions of the Fathers disagree with Scripture, we reverently bear with them and acknowledge them to be our elders. Nevertheless, we do not depart from the authority of Scripture for their sake.[3]

Today's church leaders. Many church leaders today do *not* accept the creation days as ordinary earth-rotation days. However, when their reasons are investigated, we find that influences from *outside* of Scripture (particularly belief in a billions-of-years-old universe) are the ultimate cause.

Again and again, such leaders admit that Genesis 1, taken in a straightforward way, seems to teach six ordinary days. But they then say that this cannot be, because of the age of the universe, or because of some other extra-biblical reason!

Consider the following representative quotes from Bible scholars who are considered to be conservative, yet do not accept the days of creation as ordinary-length days:

> From a superficial reading of Genesis 1, the impression would seem to be that the entire creative process took place in six twenty-four-hour days. ... This seems to run counter to modern scientific research, which indicates that the planet Earth was created several billion years ago.[4]

> We have shown the possibility of God's having formed the Earth and its life in a series of creative days representing long periods. In view of the apparent age of the Earth, this is not only possible—it is probable.[5]

It is as if these theologians view "nature" as a "67th book of the Bible," albeit with more authority than the 66 written books. Consider the words of Charles Haddon Spurgeon in 1877:

> We are invited, brethren, most earnestly to go away from the old-fashioned belief of our forefathers because of the supposed discoveries of science. What is science? The method by which man tries to conceal his ignorance. It should not be so, but so it is. You are not to be dogmatical in theology, my brethren, it is wicked; but for scientific men it is the correct thing. You are never to assert anything

very strongly; but scientists may boldly assert what they cannot prove, and may demand a faith far more credulous than any we possess. Forsooth, you and I are to take our Bibles and shape and mould our belief according to the ever-shifting teachings of so-called scientific men. What folly is this! Why, the march of science, falsely so called, through the world may be traced by exploded fallacies and abandoned theories. Former explorers once adored are now ridiculed; the continual wreckings of false hypotheses is a matter of universal notoriety. You may tell where the learned have encamped by the debris left behind of suppositions and theories as plentiful as broken bottles.[6]

C.H. Spurgeon

Those who would use historical science (as propounded by people who, by and large, ignore God's written revelation) to interpret the Bible, to teach us things about God, have matters back to front. Because we are fallen, fallible creatures, we need God's written Word, illuminated by the Holy Spirit, to properly understand natural history. The respected systematic theologian Berkhof said:

> Since the entrance of sin into the world, man can gather true knowledge about God from His general revelation only if he studies it in the light of Scripture, in which the elements of God's original self-revelation, which were obscured and perverted by the blight of sin, are republished, corrected, and interpreted. ... Some are inclined to speak of God's general revelation as a second source; but this is hardly correct in view of the fact that nature can come into consideration here only as interpreted in the light of Scripture.[7]

In other words, Christians should build their thinking on the Bible, not on "science."

The "Days" of Genesis 1

What does the Bible tell us about the meaning of "day" in Genesis 1? A word can have more than one meaning, depending on the context. For instance, the English word "day" can have perhaps 14 different meanings. For example, consider the following sentence: "Back in my father's day, it took ten days to drive across the Australian Outback during the day." Here the first occurrence of "day" means "time" in a general sense. The second "day," where a number is used, refers to an ordinary day, and the third refers to the daylight portion of the 24-hour period. The point is that words can have more than one meaning, depending on the context.

To understand the meaning of "day" in Genesis 1, we need to determine how the Hebrew word for "day," *yom*, is used in the context of Scripture. Consider the following:

- A typical concordance will illustrate that *yom* can have a range of meanings: a period of light as contrasted to night; a 24-hour period; time; a specific point of time; or a year.

- A classical, well-respected Hebrew-English lexicon[8] (a one-way dictionary) has seven headings and many subheadings for the meaning of *yom*—but it defines the creation days of Genesis 1 as ordinary days under the heading "day as defined by evening and morning."

- A number and the phrase "evening and morning" are used for each of the six days of creation (Gen. 1:5, 8, 13, 19, 23, 31).

- Outside Genesis 1, *yom* is used with a number 410 times, and each time it means an ordinary day.[9] Why would Genesis 1 be the exception?[10]

- Outside Genesis 1, *yom* is used with the word "evening" or "morning"[11] 23 times. "Evening" and "morning" appear in association, but without *yom*, 38 times. All 61 times the text refers to an ordinary day. Why would Genesis 1 be the exception?[12]

- In Genesis 1:5, *yom* occurs in context with the word "night." Outside of Genesis 1, "night" is used with *yom* 53 times—and each time it means an ordinary day. Why would Genesis 1 be the exception? Even the usage of the word "light" with *yom* in this passage determines the meaning as ordinary day.[13]

- The plural of *yom*, which does not appear in Genesis 1, *can* be used to communicate a longer time period, e.g. "in those days."[14] Adding a number here would be nonsensical. Clearly, in Exodus 20:11, where a number is used with "days," it unambiguously refers to six earth-rotation days.

- There are words in biblical Hebrew (such as *olam* or *qedem*) that are very suitable for communicating long periods of time, or indefinite time, but *none* of these words are used in Genesis 1.[15] Alternatively, the days or years could have been compared with grains of sand if long periods were meant.

Dr. James Barr (Regius Professor of Hebrew at Oxford University), who himself does not believe Genesis is true history, nonetheless admitted as far as the language of Genesis 1 is concerned that:

> So far as I know, there is no professor of Hebrew or Old Testament at any world-class university who does not believe that the writer(s) of Gen. 1–11 intended to convey to their readers the ideas that (a) creation took place in a series of six days which were the same as the days of 24 hours we now experience (b) the figures contained in the Genesis genealogies provided by simple addition a chronology from the beginning of the world up to later stages in the biblical story (c) Noah's Flood was understood to be worldwide and extinguish all human and animal life except for those in the ark.[16]

In like manner, 19th century liberal Professor Marcus Dods, New College, Edinburgh, said:

> If, for example, the word "day" in these chapters does not mean a period of twenty-four hours, the interpretation of Scripture is hopeless.[17]

Conclusion about "day" in Genesis 1

If we are prepared to let the words of the language speak to us in accord with the context and normal definitions, without being influenced by outside ideas, then the word for "day" found in Genesis 1—which is qualified by a number, the phrase "evening and morning" and for Day 1 the words "light and darkness"—*obviously* means an ordinary day (about 24 hours).

In Martin Luther's day, some of the church fathers were saying that God created everything in only one day, or in an instant. Martin Luther wrote:

> When Moses writes that God created Heaven and Earth and whatever is in them in six days, then let this period continue to have been six days, and do not venture to devise any comment according to which six days were one day. But, if you cannot understand how this could have been done in six days, then grant the Holy Spirit the honor of

Martin Luther

being more learned than you are. For you are to deal with Scripture in such a way that you bear in mind that God Himself says what is written. But since God is speaking, it is not fitting for you wantonly to turn His Word in the direction you wish to go.[18]

Similarly, John Calvin stated, "Albeit the duration of the world, now declining to its ultimate end, has not yet attained six thousand years. ... God's work was completed not in a moment but in six days."[19]

Luther and Calvin were the backbone of the Protestant Reformation that called the church back to Scripture—*Sola Scriptura* (Scripture alone). Both of these men were adamant that Genesis 1 taught six ordinary days of creation—only thousands of years ago.

John Calvin

Why six days?

Exodus 31:12 says that God commanded Moses to say to the children of Israel:

Six days may work be done, but on the seventh is the sabbath of rest, holy to the Lord. Whoever does any work in the Sabbath day, he shall surely be put to death. Therefore the sons of Israel shall keep the Sabbath, to observe the Sabbath throughout their generations, for an everlasting covenant. It is a sign between me and the sons of Israel forever. For in six days the Lord made the heavens and the earth, and on the seventh day He rested, and was refreshed (Exodus 31:15–17).

Then God gave Moses two tablets of stone upon which were written the commandments of God, written by the finger of God (Exodus 31:18).

Because God is infinite in power and wisdom, there's no doubt He could have created the universe and its contents in no time at all, or six seconds, or six minutes or six hours—after all, with God nothing shall be impossible (Luke 1:37).

13

However, the question to ask is "Why did God take so long? Why as long as six days?" The answer is also given in Exodus 20:11, and that answer is the basis of the Fourth Commandment:

> For in six days the Lord made the heavens and the earth, the sea, and all that is in them, and rested the seventh day. Therefore the Lord blessed the Sabbath day, and sanctified it.

The seven-day week has no basis outside of Scripture. In this Old Testament passage, God commands His people, Israel, to work for six days and rest for one—thus giving us a reason why He deliberately took as long as six days to create everything. He set the example for man. Our week is patterned after this principle. Now if He created everything in six thousand, or six million years, followed by a rest of one thousand or one million years, then we would have a very interesting week indeed!

Some say that Exodus 20:11 is only an analogy in the sense that man is to work and rest—not that it was to mean six literal ordinary days followed by one literal ordinary day. However, Bible scholars have shown that this commandment "does not use analogy or archetypal thinking but that its emphasis is 'stated in terms of the imitation of God or a divine precedent that is to be followed.'"[20] In other words, it was to be six literal days of work, followed by one literal day of rest, just as God worked for six literal days and rested for one.

Some have argued that "the heavens and the earth" is just earth and perhaps the solar system, not the whole universe. However, this verse clearly says that God made *everything* in six days—six consecutive ordinary days, just like the commandment in the previous verse to work for six consecutive ordinary days.

The phrase "heaven(s) and earth" in Scripture is an example of a figure of speech called a *merism*, where two opposites are combined into an all-encompassing single concept, in this case the totality of creation. A linguistic analysis of the words "heaven(s) and earth" in Scripture shows that they refer to the totality of all creation (the Hebrews did not have a word for "universe"). For example, in Genesis 14:19 God is called "Creator of heaven and earth." In Jeremiah 23:24 God speaks of himself as filling "heaven and earth." See also Genesis 14:22; 2 Kings 19:15; 2 Chronicles 2:12; Psalms 115:15, 121:2, 124:8, 134:3, 146:6; and Isaiah 37:16.

Thus, there is no scriptural warrant for restricting Exodus 20:11 to earth and its atmosphere, or the solar system alone. So Exodus 20:11 does show that the whole universe was created in six ordinary days.

Implication

As the days of creation are ordinary days in length, then by adding up the years in Scripture (assuming no gaps in the genealogies[21]), the age of the universe is only about six thousand years.[22]

REFUTING COMMON OBJECTIONS TO SIX LITERAL DAYS

Objection 1

"Science" has shown the earth and universe are billions of years old; therefore the "days" of creation must be long periods (or indefinite periods) of time.

Answer

a. The age of the earth, as determined by man's fallible methods, is based on unproven assumptions, so it is not proven that the earth is billions of years old.[23]

b. This unproven age is being used to force an interpretation on the language of the Bible. Thus, man's fallible theories are allowed to interpret the Bible. This ultimately undermines the use of language to communicate.

c. Evolutionary scientists claim the fossil layers over the earth's surface date back hundreds of millions of years. As soon as one allows millions of years for the fossil layers, then one has accepted death, bloodshed, disease, thorns, and suffering before Adam's sin.

The Bible makes it clear[24] that death, bloodshed, disease, thorns, and suffering are a *consequence* of sin.[25] In Genesis 1:29–30, God gave Adam and Eve and the animals plants to eat (this is reading Genesis at face value, as literal history, as Jesus did in Matthew 19:3–6). In fact, there is a theological distinction made between animals and plants. Human beings and higher animals are described in Genesis 1 as having a *nephesh,* or life principle. (This is true of at least the vertebrate land animals, as well as the birds and fish: Genesis 1:20, 24.) Plants do not have this *nephesh*—they are not "alive" in the same sense animals are. They were given for food.

Man was permitted to eat meat only after the Flood (Genesis 9:3)—this also makes it obvious that the statements in Genesis 1:29–30 were meant to inform us that man and the animals were vegetarian to start with. Also, in Genesis 9:2, we are told of a change God made in the way animals react to man.

God warned Adam in Genesis 2:17 that "in the day that" he ate of the "tree of the knowledge of good and evil" he would die. While Adam and Eve died spiritually immediately after eating the fruit, Romans 5:12 and 1 Cor. 15:21 show that physical death was also the consequence of Adam's sin.

After Adam disobeyed God, the Lord clothed Adam and Eve with "coats of skins" (Genesis 3:21).[26] To do this He must have killed, and shed the blood of, at least one animal. The reason for this can be summed up by Hebrews 9:22:

> And almost all things are by the law purged with blood; and without shedding of blood is no remission.

God requires the shedding of blood for the remission of sins. What happened in the Garden was a picture of what was to come in

Jesus Christ, who shed His blood on the Cross as the Lamb of God who takes away the sin of the world (John 1:29).

Now if the Garden of Eden were sitting on a fossil record of dead things millions of years old, then there was the shedding of blood *before* sin. This would destroy the foundation of the Atonement. The Bible is clear: the sin of Adam brought death and suffering into the world. As Romans 8:19–22 tells us, the whole of creation "groans" because of the effects of the fall of Adam, and the creation will be liberated "from the bondage of corruption into the glorious liberty of the children of God" (Rom. 8:21). Also, bear in mind that thorns came into existence after the Curse. Because there are thorns in the fossil record, it had to be formed after Adam and Eve sinned.

The pronouncement of the death penalty on Adam was both a curse and a blessing. A curse because death is horrible and continually reminds us of the ugliness of sin; a blessing because it meant the consequences of sin—separation from fellowship with God—need not be eternal. Death stopped Adam and his descendants from living in a state of sin, with all its consequences, forever. And because death was the just penalty for sin, Jesus Christ suffered physical death, shedding His blood, to release Adam's descendants from the consequences of sin. The Apostle Paul discusses this in depth in Romans 5, and 1 Corinthians 15.

Revelation 21–22 makes it clear that there will be a "new heavens and a new Earth" one day, where there will be "no more death" and "no more curse"—just as it was before sin changed everything. If there are to be animals as part of the new earth, obviously they will not be dying or eating each other, nor eating the redeemed people!

Thus, adding the supposed millions of years to Scripture destroys the foundations of the message of the Cross.

Objection 2

> According to Genesis 1, the sun was not created until Day 4. How could there be day and night (ordinary days) without the sun for the first three days?

Answer

a. Again, it is important for us to let the language of God's Word speak to us. If we come to Genesis 1 without any outside influences, as has been shown, each of the six days of creation appears with the Hebrew word *yom* qualified by a number and the phrase "evening and morning." The first three days are written the *same* way as the next three. So if we let the language speak to us—all six days were ordinary earth days.

b. The sun is not needed for day and night! What is needed is light and a rotating earth. On the first day of creation, God made light (Genesis 1:3). The phrase "evening and morning" certainly implies a rotating earth. Thus, if we have light from one direction, and a spinning earth, there can be day and night.

Where did the light come from? We are not told,[27] but Genesis 1:3 certainly indicates it was a created light to provide day and night until God made the sun on Day 4 to rule the day He had made. Revelation 21:23 tells us that one day the sun will not be needed, as the glory of God will light the heavenly city.

Perhaps one reason God did it this way was to illustrate that the sun did not have the priority in the creation that people have tended to give it. The sun did not give birth to the earth as evolutionary theories postulate; the sun was God's created tool to rule the day that God had made (Genesis 1:16).

Down through the ages, people such as the Egyptians have worshiped the sun. God warned the Israelites, in Deuteronomy 4:19, not to worship the sun as the pagan cultures around them did. They were commanded to worship the God who made the sun—not the sun that was *made* by God.

Evolutionary theories (the "big bang" hypothesis for instance) state that the sun came before the earth, and that the sun's energy on the earth eventually gave rise to life. Just as in pagan beliefs, the sun is, in a sense, given credit for the wonder of creation.

It is interesting to contrast the speculations of modern cosmology with the writings of the early church father Theophilus:

> On the fourth day the luminaries came into existence. Since God has foreknowledge, he understood the nonsense of the foolish philosophers who were going to say that the things produced on Earth came from the stars, so that they might set God aside. In order therefore that the truth might be demonstrated, plants and seeds came into existence before stars. For what comes into existence later cannot cause what is prior to it.[28]

Objection 3

2 Peter 3:8 states that "one day is with the Lord as a thousand years," therefore the days of creation could be long periods of time.

Answer

a. This passage has *no* creation context—it is *not* referring to Genesis or the six days of creation.

b. This verse has what is called a "comparative article"—"as" or "like"—which is not found in Genesis 1. In other words, it is *not* saying a day *is* a thousand years—it is comparing a real, literal day to a real, literal thousand years. The context of this passage is the Second Coming of Christ. It is saying that, to God, a day is *like* a thousand years, because God is outside of time. God is not limited by natural processes and time as humans are. What may seem like a long time to us (e.g., waiting for the Second Coming), or a short time, is nothing to God, either way.

c. The second part of the verse reads "and a thousand years as one day," which, in essence, cancels out the first part of the verse for those who want to equate a day with a thousand years! Thus, it cannot be saying a day is a thousand years or vice versa.

d. Psalm 90:4 states, "For a thousand years in your sight are as yesterday when it is past, and as a watch in the night." Here a thousand years is being compared with a "watch in the night" (four hours[29]). Because the phrase "watch in the night" is joined in a particular way to "yesterday," it is saying that a thousand years is being compared with a short period of time—not simply to a day.

e. If one used this passage to claim that "day" in the Bible means a thousand years, then, to be consistent, one would have to say that Jonah was in the belly of the fish three thousand years, or that Jesus has not yet risen from the dead!

Jonah—3,000 years in the whale?

Objection 4

Insisting on six solar days for creation limits God, whereas allowing God billions of years does not limit Him.

Answer

Actually, insisting on six ordinary earth-rotation days of creation is not limiting *God,* but limiting *us* to believing that God actually did what He tells us in His Word. Also, if God created everything in six days, as the Bible says, then surely this reveals the power and wisdom of God in a profound way—Almighty God did not *need* eons of time! However, the billions of years scenarios diminish God by suggesting that mere chance could create things, or that God needed huge amounts of time to create things.

Objection 5

Adam could not have accomplished all that the Bible states in one day (Day 6). He could not have named all the animals, for instance; there was not enough time.

Answer

Adam did not have to name *all* the animals—only those God brought to him. For instance,

Adam was commanded to name "every beast of the field" (Genesis 2:20), not "beast of the earth" (Genesis 1:25). The phrase "beast of the field" is most likely a subset of the larger group "beast of the earth." He did not have to name "everything that creeps upon the earth" (Genesis 1:25) or any of the sea creatures. Also the number of "kinds" would be much less than the number of "species" in today's classification.[30]

When critics say that Adam could not name the animals in less than one day, what they really mean is they do not understand how *they* could do it, so Adam could not. However, our brain has suffered from 6,000 years of the Curse—it has been greatly affected by the Fall. Before sin, Adam's brain was perfect.

When God made Adam, He must have programmed him with a perfect language. Today we program computers to "speak" and "remember." How much more could our Creator God have created Adam as a mature human (he was not born as a baby needing to learn to speak), having in his memory cells a perfect language with a perfect understanding of each word. (That is why Adam understood what God meant when he said he would "die" if he disobeyed, even though he had not seen any death.) Adam may also have had a "perfect" memory (something like a photographic memory, perhaps).

It would have been no problem for this first perfect man to make up words and name the animals God brought to him and remember the names—in far less than one day.[31]

Objection 6

Genesis 2 is a different account of creation, with a different order, so how can the first chapter be accepted as teaching six literal days?

Answer

Actually, Genesis 2 is not a *different* account of creation. It is a *more detailed* account of Day 6 of creation. Chapter 1 is an overview of the whole of creation; chapter 2 gives details surrounding the creation of the Garden, the first man and his activities on Day 6.[32]

Between the creation of Adam and the creation of Eve, the King James Version says, "Out of the ground the Lord God formed every beast of the field and every fowl of the air" (Genesis 2:19). This seems to say that the land beasts and birds were created between the creation of Adam and

Eve. However, Jewish scholars did not recognize any such conflict with the account in chapter 1, where Adam and Eve were both created after the beasts and birds (Genesis 1:23–25). There is no contradiction, because in Hebrew the precise tense of a verb is determined by the context. It is clear from chapter 1 that the beasts and birds were created before Adam, so Jewish scholars would have understood the verb "formed," in Genesis 2:19, to mean "had formed" or "having formed." If we translate verse 19 "Now the Lord God had formed out of the ground all the beasts of the field," the apparent disagreement with Genesis 1 disappears completely.

Regarding the plants and herbs in Genesis 2:5 and the trees in Genesis 2:9 (compare with Genesis 1:12), the plants and herbs are described as "of the field" and they needed a man to tend them. These are clearly cultivated plants, not just plants in general (Genesis 1). Also, the trees (Genesis 2:9) are only the trees planted in the Garden, not trees in general.

In Matthew 19:3–6 Jesus Christ quotes from both Genesis 1:27 and Genesis 2:24 when referring to the *same man and woman* in teaching the doctrine of marriage. Clearly, Jesus saw them as *complementary* accounts, *not* contradictory ones.

Objection 7

> There is no "evening and morning" for the seventh day of the creation week (Genesis 2:2). Thus, we must still be in the "seventh day," so none of the days can be ordinary days.

Answer

Look again at the previous section, entitled "Why six days?" Exodus 20:11 is clearly referring to seven literal days—six for work and one for rest.

Also, God stated that He *"rested"* from His work of creation (not that He *is resting*!). The fact that He rested from His work of creation does not preclude Him from continuing to rest from this activity. God's work now is different— it is a work of sustaining His creation, and of reconciliation and redemption because of man's sin.

The word *yom* is qualified by a number (Genesis 2:2–3), so the context still determines that it is an ordinary solar day. Also, God blessed this seventh day and made it holy. In Genesis 3:17–19 we read of the Curse on the earth because of sin. Paul refers to this in Romans 8:22. It does

30

not make sense that God would call this day holy and blessed if He cursed the ground on this "day." We live in a sin-cursed earth—we are not in the seventh blessed holy day!

Note: In arguing that the seventh day is not an ordinary day because it is not associated with "evening and morning" like the other days, proponents are tacitly agreeing that the other six days are ordinary days because they are defined by an evening and a morning!

Some have argued that Hebrews 4:3–4 implies that the seventh day is continuing today. However, verse 4 reiterates that God rested (past tense) on the seventh day. If someone says on Monday that he rested on Friday and is still resting, this would not suggest that Friday continued through to Monday! Also, only those who have believed in Christ will enter that rest, showing that it is a spiritual rest, which is compared with God's rest since the creation week. It is not some sort of continuation of the seventh day (otherwise *everyone* would be "in" this rest).[33]

Hebrews does *not* say that the seventh day of creation week is continuing today, merely that the rest He instituted is continuing.

Objection 8

> *Genesis 2:4 states, "In the day that the Lord God made the earth and the heavens." As this refers to all six days of creation, it shows that the word "day" does not mean an ordinary day.*

Answer

The Hebrew word *yom* as used here is *not* qualified by a number, the phrase "evening and morning," or light or darkness. In this context, the verse really means "in the time God created" (referring to the creation week) or "when God created."

Other problems with long days and similar interpretations

- If the plants made on Day 3 were separated by millions of years from the birds and nectar bats (created Day 5), and insects (created Day 6) necessary for their pollination, then such plants could not have survived. This problem would be especially acute for species with complex symbiotic relationships (each depending on the other; e.g., the yucca plant and the associated moth[34]).

- Adam was created on Day 6, lived through Day 7, and then died when he was 930 years old (Genesis 5:5). If each day were a thousand years, or millions of years, this would make no sense of Adam's age at death!

- Some have claimed that the word for "made" (*asah*) in Exodus 20:11 actually means "show." They propose that God showed or revealed the information about creation to Moses during a six-day period. This allows for the creation itself to have occurred over millions of years.

However, "showed" is not a valid translation for *asah*. Its meaning covers "to make, manufacture, produce, do," etc., but not "to show" in the sense of reveal.[35] Where *asah* is translated as "show"—for example, "show kindness" (Genesis 24:12)—it is in the sense of "to do" or "make" kindness.

- Some have claimed that because the word *asah* is used for the creation of the sun, moon, and stars on Day 4, and not the word *bara,* which is used in Genesis 1:1 for "create," this means God only revealed the sun, moon, and stars at this stage. They insist the word *asah* has the meaning of "revealed." In other words, the luminaries were supposedly already in existence, and were only revealed at this stage. However, *bara* and *asah* are used in Scripture to describe the same event. For example, *asah* is used in Exodus 20:11 to refer to the creation of the heavens and the earth, but *bara* is used to refer to the creation of the heavens and the earth in Genesis 1:1. The word *asah* is used concerning the creation of the first people in Genesis 1:26—they did not previously exist. And then they are said to have been created *(bara)* in Genesis 1:27. There are many other similar examples. *Asah* has a broad range of meanings involving "to do" or "to make," which includes *bara* creation.

- Some accept that the days of creation are ordinary days as far as the language of Genesis is concerned, but not as literal days of history as far as man is concerned. This is basically the view called the "framework hypothesis."[36] This is a very complex and contrived view which has been thoroughly refuted by scholars.[37]

The real purpose of the "framework hypothesis" can be seen in the following quote from an article by one of its proponents:

> To rebut the literalist interpretation of the Genesis creation "week" propounded by the young-earth theorists is a central concern of this article.[38]

- Some people want the days of creation to be long periods in an attempt to harmonize evolution or billions of years with the Bible's account of origins. However, the order of events according to long-age beliefs does not agree with that of Genesis. Consider the following table:

Contradictions between the order of creation in the Bible and evolution/day-ages

Biblical Account of Creation	Evolutionary/long-age speculation
Earth before the sun and stars	Stars and sun before earth
Earth covered in water initially	Earth a molten blob initially
Oceans first, then dry land	Dry land, then the oceans
Life first created on the land	Life started in the oceans
Plants created before the sun	Plants came long after the sun
Land animals created after birds	Land animals existed before birds
Whales before land animals	Land animals before whales

Clearly, those who do not accept the six literal days are the ones reading their own preconceived ideas into the passage.

Long-age compromises

Other than the "gap theory" (the belief that there is a gap of indeterminate time between the first two verses of Genesis 1), the major compromise positions that try to harmonize long ages and/or evolution with Genesis fall into two categories:

1. "theistic evolution" wherein God supposedly directed the evolutionary process of millions of years, or even just set it up and let it run, and

2. "progressive creation" where God supposedly

intervened in the processes of death and
struggle for survival to create millions of species
at various times over millions of years.

All long-age compromises reject Noah's Flood as
a global Flood—it could only be a local event,
because the fossil layers are accepted as evidence
for millions of years. A global Flood would have
destroyed this record and produced another!
Therefore, these positions cannot allow a catastrophic global Flood that would form layers
of fossil-bearing rocks over the earth. This, of
course, goes against Scripture, which obviously
teaches a global Flood (Genesis 6–9).[38]

Does it really matter?

Yes, it does matter what a Christian believes
concerning the days of creation in Genesis 1.
Most importantly, all schemes which insert eons
of time into, or before, creation undermine the
gospel by putting death, bloodshed, disease,
thorns, and suffering before sin and the Fall, as
explained above (see answer to Objection 1).
Here are two more reasons:

1. It is really a matter of how one approaches
   the Bible, in principle. If we do not allow the

language to speak to us in context, but try to make the text fit ideas outside of Scripture, then ultimately the meaning of any word in any part of the Bible depends on man's interpretation—which can change according to whatever outside ideas are in vogue.

2. If one allows "science" (which has wrongly become synonymous with evolution and materialism) to determine our understanding of Scripture, then this can lead to a slippery slope of unbelief through the rest of Scripture. For instance, "science" would proclaim that a person cannot be raised from the dead. Does this mean we should "interpret" the Resurrection of Christ to reflect this? Sadly, some do just this, saying that the Resurrection simply means that Jesus' teachings live on in His followers!

When people accept at face value what Genesis is teaching, and accept the days as ordinary days, they will have no problem accepting and making sense of the rest of the Bible.

Martin Luther once said:

> I have often said that whoever would study Holy Scripture should be sure to see to it

that he stays with the simple words as long as he can and by no means departs from them unless an article of faith compels him to understand them differently. For of this we must be certain: no clearer speech has been heard on Earth than what God has spoken.[39]

Pure words

God's people need to realize that the Word of God is something very special. It is not just the words of men. As Paul said in 1 Thessalonians 2:13, "You received it not as the word of men, but as it is, truly the word of God."

Proverbs 30:5–6 states that "every word of God is pure … . Do not add to His words, lest He reprove you and you be found a liar." The Bible cannot be treated as just some great literary work. We need to "tremble at his word" (Isaiah 6:5) and not forget:

> All Scripture is God-breathed, and is profitable for doctrine, for reproof, for correction, for instruction in righteousness, that the man of God may be perfected, thoroughly equipped for every good work (2 Timothy 3:16–17).

In the original autographs, every word and letter in the Bible is there because God put it there. Let us listen to God speaking to us through His Word, and not arrogantly think we can tell God what He really means!

Here's the Good News

Answers in Genesis seeks to give glory and honor to God as Creator, and to affirm the truth of the biblical record of the real origin and history of the world and mankind.

Part of this real history is the bad news that the rebellion of the first man, Adam, against God's command brought death, suffering, and separation from God into this world. We see the results all around us. All of Adam's descendants are sinful from conception (Psalm 51:5) and have themselves entered into this rebellion (sin). They therefore cannot live with a holy God, but are condemned to separation from God. The Bible says that "all have sinned, and come short of the glory of God" (Romans 3:23) and that all are therefore subject to "everlasting destruction from the presence of the Lord and from the glory of His power" (2 Thessalonians 1:9).

But the good news is that God has done something about it. "For God so loved the world, that He gave his only-begotten Son, that whoever believes in Him should not perish, but have everlasting life" (John 3:16).

Jesus Christ the Creator, though totally sinless, suffered, on behalf of mankind, the penalty of mankind's sin, which is death and separation from God. He did this to satisfy the righteous demands of the holiness and justice of God, His Father. Jesus was the perfect sacrifice; He died on a cross, but on the third day, He rose again, conquering death, so that all who truly believe in Him, repent of their sin and trust in Him (rather than their own merit) are able to come back to God and live for eternity with their Creator.

Therefore; "He who believes on Him is not condemned, but he who does not believe is condemned already, because he has not believed in the name of the only-begotten Son of God" (John 3:18).

What a wonderful Savior—and what a wonderful salvation in Christ our Creator!

(If you want to know more of what the Bible

says about how you can receive eternal life, please write or call the Answers in Genesis office nearest you—see inside front cover.)

References

1. Van Bebber, M. and Taylor, P., *Creation and Time: A Report on the Progressive Creationist Book by Hugh Ross*, Films for Christ, Mesa, Arizona, 1994.

2. Hasel, G., The "days" of Creation in Genesis 1: literal "days" or figurative "periods/epochs" of time? *Origins* **21**(1):5–38, 1994.

3. M. Luther as cited in Plass, E., *What Martin Luther Says: A Practical In-Home Anthology for the Active Christian,* Concordia Publishing House, St Louis, p. 1523, 1991.

4. Archer, G., *A Survey of Old Testament Introduction,* Moody Press, Chicago, pp. 196–197, 1994.

5. Boice, J., *Genesis: An Expositional Commentary,* Vol. 1, Genesis 1:1–11, Zondervan Publishing House, Grand Rapids, Michigan, p. 68, 1982.

6. Spurgeon, C., *The Sword and the Trowel,* p. 197, 1877.

7. Berkhof, L., introductory volume to *Systematic Theology,* Wm. B. Eerdsmans, Grand Rapids, Michigan, pp. 60, 96, 1946.

8. Brown, F., Driver, S. and Briggs, C., *A Hebrew and English Lexicon of the Old Testament,* Clarendon Press, Oxford, p. 398, 1951.

9. Some say that Hosea 6:2 is an exception to this because of the figurative language. However, the Hebrew idiomatic expression used, "After two days ... in the third day," meaning "in a short time," makes sense only if "day" is understood in its normal sense.

10. Stambaugh, J., The days of Creation: a semantic

    approach, *Proc. Evangelical Society's Far West Region Meeting,* Master's Seminary, Sun Valley, California, p. 12, 26 April 1996.

11. The Jews start their day in the evening (sundown followed by night)—obviously based on the fact that Genesis begins the day with the "evening."

12. Stambaugh, Ref. 10, p. 15.

13. Stambaugh, Ref. 10, p. 72.

14. Stambaugh, Ref. 10, pp. 72–73.

15. Stambaugh, Ref. 10, pp. 73–74.

    Grigg, R., How long were the days of Genesis 1? *Creation* **19**(1):23–25, 1996.

16. Barr, J., Letter to David Watson, 23 April 1984.

17. Dods, M., *Expositor's Bible,* T & T Clark, Edinburgh, p. 4, 1888, as cited by Kelly, D., *Creation and Change,* Christian Focus Publications, Fearn, Scotland, p. 112, 1997.

18. Plass, Ref. 3, p. 1523.

19. McNeil, J. (Ed.), *Calvin: Institutes of the Christian Religion 1,* Westminster Press, Louisville, Kentucky, pp. 160–161, 182, 1960.

20. Hasel, Ref. 2, p. 29.

21. Whitcomb, J. and Morris, H., *The Genesis Flood,* Presbyterian and Reformed Publ., Phillipsburg, New Jersey, USA, pp. 481–483, 1961, Appendix II. They allow for the possibility of gaps in the genealogies because the word "begat" can skip generations. However, they point out that even allowing for gaps would

give a maximum age of around 10,000 years.

22. Pierce, L., The forgotten archbishop, *Creation* **20**(2):42–43, 1998. Ussher carried out a very scholarly work in adding up all the years in Scripture to obtain a date of creation of 4004 BC. Ussher has been mocked for stating that creation occurred on 23 October—he obtained this date by working backwards using the Jewish civil year and accounting for how the year and month were derived over the years. Thus, he didn't just pull this date out of the air, but gave a scholarly mathematical basis for it. This is not to say this is the correct date, as there are assumptions involved, but the point is, his work is not to be scoffed at. Ussher did *not* specify the hour of the day for creation as some skeptics assert. Young's *Analytical Concordance*, under "creation," lists many other authorities, including extra-biblical ones, who all give a date for creation of less than 10,000 years ago.

23. Morris, H. and Morris, J., *Science, Scripture, and the Young Earth,* Institute for Creation Research, El Cajon, California, pp. 39–44, 1989.

    Morris, J., *The Young Earth,* Master Books, Green Forest, Arkansas, pp. 51–67, 1996.

    Austin, S., *Grand Canyon: Monument to Catastrophe,* Institute for Creation Research, El Cajon, California, pp. 111–131, 1994.

    Humphreys, D., *Starlight and Time,* Appendix C, Master Books, Green Forest, Arkansas, 1996.

    Progress towards a young-earth relativistic cosmology, *Proc. 3rd ICC,* Pittsburg, pp. 83–133, 1994.

Wieland, C., Creation in the physics lab (interview with Dr. Russell Humphreys), *Creation* **15**(3):20–23, 1993.

Taylor, I., *In the Minds of Men,* TFE Publ., Toronto, pp. 295–322, 1984.

24. Ham, K., *The Lie: Evolution,* Master Books, Green Forest, Arkansas, Introduction, pp. xiii–xiv, 1987.

Ham, K., The necessity for believing in six literal days, *Creation* **18**(1):38–41, 1996.

Ham, K., The wrong way round! *Creation* **18**(3):38–41, 1996.

Ham, K., Fathers, promises and vegemite, *Creation* **19**(1):14–17, 1997.

Ham, K., The narrow road, *Creation* **19**(2):47–49, 1997.

Ham, K., Millions of years and the "doctrine of Balaam," *Creation* **19**(3):15–17, 1997.

25. Gill, J., *A Body of Doctrinal and Practical Divinity,* 1760. Republished by Primitive Baptist Library, p. 191, 1980. This is not just a new idea from modern scholars. In 1760 John Gill, in his commentaries, insisted there was no death, bloodshed, disease or suffering before sin.

26. All Eve's progeny, except the God-man Jesus Christ, were born with original sin (Romans 5:12, 18–19), so Eve could not have conceived when she was sinless. So the Fall must have occurred fairly quickly, before Eve had conceived any children (they were told to "be fruitful and multiply").

27. Some people ask why God did not tell us the source

of this light. However, if God told us everything, we would have so many books we would not have time to read them. God has given us all the information we need to come to the right conclusions about the things that really matter.

28. Lavallee, L., The early church defended creation science, *Impact,* No. 160, p. ii, 1986. Quotation from *Theophilus, "To Autolycus,"* 2.8, Oxford Early Christian Texts.

29. The Jews had three watches during the night (sunset to 10 pm; 10 pm to 2 am; 2 am to sunrise), but the Romans had four watches, beginning at 6 pm.

30. Ham, K. *et al., The Answers Book,* Master Books, Green Forest, Arkansas, pp. 180–182, 2000.

31. Grigg, R., Naming the animals: all in a day's work for Adam, *Creation* **18**(4):46–49, 1996.

32. Batten, D., Genesis contradictions? *Creation* **18**(4):44–45, 1996.

    Kruger, M., An understanding of Genesis 2:5, *CEN Technical Journal* **11**(1):106–110, 1997.

33. Anon., Is the Seventh Day an eternal day? *Creation* **21**(3):44–45, 1999.

34. Meldau, F., *Why We Believe in Creation Not in Evolution,* Christian Victory Publ., Denver, Colorado, pp. 114–116, 1972.

35. Nothing in Gesenius's *Lexicon* supports the interpretation of *asah* as "show."

    See Charles Taylor's "Days of Revelation or creation?" (1997) found on the Answers in Genesis website, www.AnswersInGenesis.org.

36. Kline, M., Because it had not rained, *Westminster Theological Journal* **20**:146–157, 1957–1958.

    Kline, M., Space and time in the Genesis cosmology, *Perspectives on Science & Christian Faith* **48**(1), 1996.

37. Kruger, Ref. 31, pp. 106–110.

    Pipa, J., From chaos to cosmos: a critique of the framework hypothesis, presented at the Far-Western Regional Annual Meeting of the Evangelical Theological Society, USA, April 26, 1996.

    Wayne Grudem's *Systematic Theology,* InterVarsity Press, Downers Grove, Illinois, USA, pp. 302–305, 1994, summarizes the framework hypothesis and its problems and inconsistencies.

38. Van Bebber and Taylor, Ref. 1, pp. 55–59.

    Whitcomb and Morris, Ref. 21, pp. 212–330.

39. Plass, Ref. 3, p. 93.

For information on AiG's "walk-though-the-Bible" Creation Museum (which is very evangelistic) located near Cincinnati, Ohio, go to: *www.CreationMuseum.org*.

Additional reading:

The Lie: Evolution—Ken Ham

The New Answers Book—Ken Ham et al.

The Young Earth—John Morris

Other booklets in this series:

What Really Happened to the Dinosaurs?—Ken Ham

Is There Really a God?—Ken Ham

Where Did Cain Get His Wife?—Ken Ham

Where Did the 'Races' Come From?—Ken Ham, Dr. Carl Wieland, Dr. Don Batten

Why Is There Death and Suffering?—Ken Ham & Mark Looy, eds.

Is There Intelligent Life in Outer Space?—Ken Ham, Dr. Don Batten

Gay Marriage: Are There Answers?—Ken Ham, Dr. Jonathan Sarfati

Was There Really a Noah's Ark & Flood?—Ken Ham

Translations:

Some of the above materials are available in other languages. Please contact the ministry nearest you for details.

Were the days of creation ordinary-length days?

How are we meant to understand the Bible?

Does Genesis 2 contradict Genesis 1?

ISBN-10 1-89334523-8
ISBN-13 978-1-89334523-2

9 781893 345232

1:1
answersingenesis.org
believing it. defending it. proclaiming it.